19

TRIANGLE HISTORIES
★★★ ★ ★★★
THE CIVIL WAR

THE BATTLE OF
GETTYSBURG

David C. King

BLACKBIRCH PRESS, INC.
WOODBRIDGE, CONNECTICUT

Published by Blackbirch Press, Inc.
260 Amity Road
Woodbridge, CT 06525

Web site: http://www.blackbirch.com
e-mail: staff@blackbirch.com

© 2001 Blackbirch Press, Inc.

Printed in China

10 9 8 7 6 5 4 3 2 1

Photo credits:
Cover, pages 9, 10 11, 13, 15, 17, 18, 19, 20, 21, 22, 24, 26, 27,28, 29: North Wind Picture Archives; page 7: Corel Corporation; page 12: National Portrait Gallery, Smithsonian Institute; page 14: Blackbirch Press; pages 16, 25: Library of Congress.

Library of Congress Cataloging-in-Publication Data
King, David C.
The Battle of Gettysburg / by David C. King.
    p. cm. — (The Civil War)
Includes index.
Summary: Discusses the strategy, tactics, actual fighting, aftermath, and key figures involved in one of the Civil War's pivotal battles at Gettysburg, Pennsylvania.
    ISBN 1-56711-550-0 (hardcover: alk. paper)
1. Gettysburg (Pa.), Battle of, 1863—Juvenile Literature. [1. Gettysburg (Pa.), Battle of, 1863. 2. United States—History—Civil War, 1861-1865—Campaigns.]
I. Title. II. Civil War (Blackbirch Press).
E475.53 .K56 2001   2001002569
973. 7349—dc21

CONTENTS

PREFACE: THE CIVIL WAR

Nearly 150 years after the final shots were fired, the Civil War remains one of the key events in U. S. history. The enormous loss of life alone makes it tragically unique: More Americans died in Civil War battles than in all other American wars combined. More Americans fell at the Battle of Gettysburg than during any battle in American military history. And, in one day at the Battle of Antietam, more Americans were killed and wounded than in any other day in American history.

As tragic as the loss of life was, however, it is the principles over which the war was fought that make it uniquely American. Those beliefs—equality and freedom—are the foundation of American democracy, our basic rights. It was the bitter disagreement about the exact nature of those rights that drove our nation to its bloodiest war.

The disagreements grew in part from the differing economies of the North and South. The warm climate and wide-open areas of the Southern states were ideal for an economy based on agriculture. In the first half of the 19th century, the main cash crop was cotton, grown on large farms called plantations. Slaves, who were brought to the United States from Africa, were forced to do the backbreaking work of planting and harvesting cotton. They also provided the other labor necessary to keep plantations running. Slaves were bought and sold like property, and had been critical to the Southern economy since the first Africans came to America in 1619.

The suffering of African Americans under slavery is one of the great tragedies in American history. And the debate over whether the United States government had the right to forbid slavery—in both Southern states and in new territories—was a dispute that overshadowed the first 80 years of our history.

For many Northerners, the question of slavery was one of morality and not economics. Because the Northern economy was based on manufacturing rather than agriculture, there was little need for slave labor. The primary economic need of Northern states was a protective tax known as a tariff that would make imported goods more expensive than goods made in the North. Tariffs forced Southerners to buy Northern goods and made them economically dependent on the North, a fact that led to deep resentment among Southerners.

4

Economic control did not matter to the anti-slavery Northerners known as abolitionists. Their conflict with the South was over slavery. The idea that the federal government could outlaw slavery was perfectly reasonable. After all, abolitionists contended, our nation was founded on the idea that all people are created equal. How could slavery exist in such a country?

For the Southern states that joined the Confederacy, the freedom from unfair taxation and the right to make their own decisions about slavery was as important a principle as equality. For most Southerners, the right of states to decide what is best for its citizens was the most important principle guaranteed in the Constitution.

The conflict over these principles generated sparks throughout the decades leading up to the Civil War. The importance of keeping an equal number of slave and free states in the Union became critical to Southern lawmakers in Congress in those years. In 1820, when Maine and Missouri sought admission to the Union, the question was settled by the Missouri Compromise: Maine was admitted as a free state, Missouri as a slave state, thus maintaining a balance in Congress. The compromise stated that all future territories north of the southern boundary of Missouri would enter the Union as free states, those south of it would be slave states.

In 1854, however, the Kansas-Nebraska Act set the stage for the Civil War. That act repealed the Missouri Compromise and, by declaring that the question of slavery should be decided by residents of the territory, set off a rush of pro- and anti-slavery settlers to the new land. Violence between the two sides began almost immediately and soon "Bleeding Kansas" became a tragic chapter in our nation's story.

With Lincoln's election on an anti-slavery platform in 1860, the disagreement over the power of the federal government reached its breaking point. South Carolina became the first state to secede from the Union, followed by Mississippi, Florida, Alabama, Georgia, Louisiana, Virginia, Texas, North Carolina, Tennessee, and Arkansas. Those eleven states became the Confederate States of America. Confederate troops fired the first shots of the Civil War at Fort Sumter, South Carolina, on April 12, 1861. Those shots began a four-year war in which thousands of Americans—Northerners and Southerners—would give, in President Lincoln's words, "the last full measure of devotion."

INTRODUCTION: VALLEY OF DEATH

★ ★ ★ ★ ★

A strange quiet had settled over the battlefield. No breeze stirred the sultry summer air. On both sides of the valley, soldiers stretched out on the grass, dozing or talking quietly. Then, at exactly 1:07 P.M., two Confederate cannons fired. Moments later, the rest of the Confederate artillery—140 guns in all—opened fire. The Rebel guns were aimed at the Union position across the valley on Cemetery Ridge. Union troops on the ridge scrambled for cover. Behind them, 80 Union cannons answered the Confederate fire.

After two days of savage fighting, the artillery barrage was the opening phase of the Confederate plan for an infantry charge across the mile-wide valley. Behind the daring plan was the desperate hope that they would break the Union line and achieve a critical victory.

The shallow valley between the two armies quickly filled with artillery smoke. The only target gunners could see to aim at were the stabs of flame from cannons firing back at them. On Cemetery Ridge, Federal troops hugged the ground as shells whined, shrieked, and howled overhead, then exploded. A Union private wrote that some shells hit ammunition wagons, sending "fragments of wheels, woodwork, shell, and shot . . . a hundred feet in the air like the eruption of a volcano."

One by one, the Union cannons stopped firing. Colonel Edward Potter, commander of the Confederate artillery, concluded that his cannons were knocking out one federal battery after another. He sent word for the crucial infantry assault to begin. Quickly, 12,000 Rebel soldiers moved out of the cover of trees and fixed their bayonets. Marching in close formation, separated by only inches from comrades on all sides, the Rebels began the march across the wide-open valley. The decisive attack of the battle—perhaps of the war—was about to begin.

THE SOUTH'S BOLD GAMBLE

In late May 1863, Confederate General Robert E. Lee made a daring move. He began preparing his army to invade Pennsylvania in an effort to carry the war onto Northern soil. He hoped that a decisive victory there would persuade Northerners that after two years of bloodshed—and numerous Southern victories—it was useless to continue fighting. He felt that a decisive victory by the South would put pressure on Union President Abraham Lincoln to seek peace.

Lee's well-trained soldiers began loading 1,000 canvas-topped army wagons with supplies, food, and ammunition. They would also be used to transport the inevitable wounded after battles. Northerners called these battle-hardened Southern troops "Rebels," and the troops accepted the label proudly. For two years, these "Rebels" had spent almost all of their time in Virginia, fighting to prevent the Northern Army of the Potomac from capturing Richmond, the capital of the Confederacy. Now, as they prepared to move into Pennsylvania, the Rebels were prepared to fight hard to protect the Southern way of life.

Many in the Confederacy, including President Jefferson Davis, wanted Lee to move most of his Army of Northern Virginia to the West, in order to help save the city of Vicksburg, Mississippi, from falling into Union hands. Vicksburg, the South's last major stronghold on the Mississippi River, was under siege by a powerful Union army commanded by General Ulysses S. Grant. If Vicksburg fell, the North would gain control of the entire Mississippi River Valley and the Confederacy would be cut in two, preventing men and supplies from reaching Confederate forces in the East.

Though Lee's plan to move north instead of west seemed radical, President Davis and his cabinet agreed to it. It was hard to refuse Lee because he had done so much to save the Confederacy. Lee's Army of Northern Virginia had won major battles at Fredericksburg in December 1862 and Chancellorsville in early May of 1863—just two weeks before his meeting with President Davis.

8

Those two victories had given Lee and his men enormous confidence. As he told President Davis and the cabinet, "There never were such men in an army before. They will go anywhere and do anything if properly led."

Into Enemy Territory

Early in June, Lee set his army into motion. He sent them in stages in order to maintain secrecy as long as possible from the Army of the Potomac, which remained camped along the Rappahannock River, located directly across from Fredericksburg. He had divided his Army of Northern Virginia into three corps, each with nearly 25,000 men. The "I Corps," commanded by General James Longstreet, moved north first, taking up positions to guard the passes through the Blue Ridge Mountains that led into the Shenandoah Valley. General Richard Ewell's "II Corps" went next. They moved through the passes, then followed the Shenandoah north toward Pennsylvania. The "III Corps," under General A.P. Hill, remained in Fredericksburg for a few days, hoping to convince the enemy that most of the Army of Northern Virginia was still there.

"There never were such men in an army before. They will go anywhere and do anything if properly led."

Robert E. Lee, speaking about his army

The Rebel troops of Lee's Army of Northern Virginia were well-trained and battle-tested fighters.

The Union Army of the Potomac, commanded by General Joseph "Fighting Joe" Hooker, was still recovering from the humiliating defeat at the Battle of Chancellorsville on May 1 and 2, 1863. That conflict had shown Lee at his most brilliant, repeatedly out-maneuvering, and eventually beating, an army that outnumbered his nearly two to one. Despite the defeat, Hooker's army remained a danger, capable of renewing the fighting at any time. By early June, Hooker became aware that at least part of the Confederate force was on the move. Following directions from President Lincoln, Hooker began moving his army northward, planning to stay between the Confederates and Washington, D.C. Hooker also sent out his cavalry division to determine Lee's intentions.

The Union defeat at Chancellorsville opened the way for Confederates to move into Pennsylvania.

In addition to the Army of Northern Virginia's three corps of infantry, Lee relied heavily on his own 10,000-man cavalry division. The commander of the cavalry was General James Ewell Brown (Jeb) Stuart, a daring and colorful officer who was one of Lee's favorites.

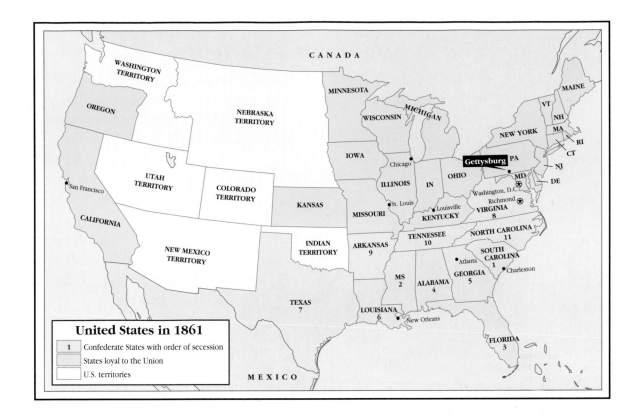

United States in 1861

1	Confederate States with order of secession
	States loyal to the Union
	U.S. territories

The two men had worked well together. Lee called Stuart his "eyes and ears," because the cavalry's main task was to keep the commander informed of the enemy's location, strengths, and movements.

Lee's invasion plan depended on knowing where the Army of the Potomac was at all times, but in this campaign, Stuart failed him. On June 25, Stuart led his cavalry in a wide circle around the Union army, but the distance and the difficulties were greater than he'd expected. As a result, Lee heard nothing from Stuart for eight days. By the time Stuart showed up, the information he carried came too late to help his commander.

By late June, the forerunners of Lee's army were in Pennsylvania, with the three corps still widely spread over an area of nearly 100 miles. As advance troops moved forward, fear and rumor rippled out ahead of them. The governor of Pennsylvania called out the state militia and, in Washington, President Lincoln called for 100,000 fresh troops.

General Jeb Stewart was Lee's most trusted cavalry commander.

The Accidental Battlefield

During the Confederates' three-week march north, General Lee had not been troubled by how spread-out his troops were. It helped to disguise their destination and also made it easier for the men to gather food. Once in Pennsylvania, he planned to bring the three corps together and march on Harrisburg, the state capital. "After that," he had told the Confederate leaders, "I can turn my attention to Philadelphia, Baltimore, or Washington as may seem best for our interests." On June 28, however, a spy delivered the shocking news that the Union army had already crossed the Potomac and was rapidly closing in on his right flank. The next day, Lee learned that Hooker had been replaced by General George Meade.

General Joseph "Fighting Joe" Hooker (above) was replaced by General George Meade as Commander of Union armies.

Lee's careful plan rapidly came apart, due in part to the failure of his cavalry commander, Stuart. Where was Stuart, Lee wondered? Why had the Confederates learned so late that the Army of the Potomac had crossed the river and was already dangerously close? Why had it taken three days to find out that the enemy had a new commander?

Lee had known the Union commander, Meade, since the Mexican War, and he respected him as a tough, no-nonsense warrior. As Lee commented to an aide, "General Meade will make no blunder on my front." Lee now knew that he had to move quickly. He sent messages to his corps commanders, telling them to move as rapidly as possible toward Cashtown and Gettysburg. He hoped to choose a battle site closer to Harrisburg, so he ordered the men not to start a general battle until he gave the word—even if they were attacked.

As the Army of the Potomac pushed westward, General Meade also advised his commanders to avoid a full-scale battle until he arrived. Meade was still stunned by his promotion to the commander of the army, and he wanted to fight from a strong defensive position, forcing the Confederates to attack him on ground that he had chosen.

As the month of June drew to a close, the long gray and blue lines of soldiers inched their way across the rolling hills and fertile farmland of Pennsylvania toward their inevitable collision. Neither commander felt quite ready to fight, and neither had chosen the town of Gettysburg. More by accident than by design, the two armies were drifting into the greatest battle of the Civil War—and one of the most memorable in the nation's history.

"General Meade will make no blunder on my front."

—*Confederate General Lee discussing his Union opponent*

Gettysburg: Day 1

On the morning of July 1, 1863, Union General John Buford led his two cavalry brigades along the Chambersburg Road outside of

The Union Army crossed the Potomac River faster than Lee expected.

General George
Meade, commander of
the Union forces,
fought in the Mexican
War with Lee.

★

Early on July 1,
Buford's Union
cavalry met Heth's
Rebel infantry
north of
Gettysburg and
were driven back
through the town.

★

Gettysburg, looking for Confederate infantry. His men
had spotted the Southerners the day before. That night
he had told his men to be ready to fight. "They will
attack you in the morning," Buford predicted, "and
they will come booming . . . . You will have to fight like
the devil until supports arrive."

As Buford's troops approached Gettysburg, they
spotted the Rebels also nearing the town. The
Confederates were part of A.P. Hill's III Corps—a
division commanded by General Henry Heth. Heth's
men had heard there was a shoe factory in town and
Heth received permission to find his men shoes, always
in short supply in the Southern armies.

Buford saw that he was badly outnumbered and sent
an urgent message for help. At the same time, he
ordered his men to dismount and open fire from the
cover of trees and fences. Heth's Rebel infantry numbered more than
7,000, while Buford's Yankees were less than 3,000, and one man out
of every four had to hold the reins for the others' horses. Despite the
numbers, the Union troops were able to hold off the Rebels for nearly
two hours, giving ground only slowly. Buford's men had one
advantage that offset the numbers—they were equipped with new
top-loading carbines. These guns enabled a trooper to squeeze off
fifteen to twenty shots per minute, compared to three or four shots
by a Confederate with a standard muzzle-loading Springfield musket.

Late in the morning, Buford's cavalry received help from a Union
division commanded by General John Reynolds. One of Reynolds' units
was the battle-tested 6th Wisconsin, known as the "Iron Brigade." They
took up positions on the edge of Gettysburg and waited for the
Confederate infantry to attack. One of the Iron Brigade men recalled:

For a mile up and down the open field before us, the splended [sic]
line of the veterans of the Army of Northern Virginia swept down upon
us. Their bearing was magnificent. They came forward with a rush, and
how our men did yell, "Come on, Johnny Reb, Come on!"

Heth's Rebels, however, were also receiving reinforcements from Ewell's II Corps. The Union troops found themselves outnumbered again. They retreated through and around Gettysburg and tried to establish a position on Culp's Hill. Another Iron Brigade soldier described the action:

"For seven or eight minutes ensued probably the most desperate fight ever waged between artillery and infantry at close range without a particle of cover on either side . . . bullets hissing, humming, and whistling everywhere; cannons roaring; all crash on crash and peal, smoke, dust, splinters, blood, wreck and carnage indescribable."

By late afternoon, the Confederates had suffered 8,000 casualties, but they had the Federals on the run. As they pushed the Northerners through the streets of Gettysburg, they felt they were on the verge of a great victory.

ABOVE: Union General John Buford
BELOW: Union General John Reynolds

General Reynolds was killed. At that point, the Yankees were close to total collapse.

Some Union men made their way to Cemetery Hill, where the arrival of another highly-respected officer—General Winfield Scott Hancock—helped to steady the men. Hancock established a defensive line, but the line was so thin, he thought this might be his last stand.

It was at this point that General Lee arrived on the scene. He was upset that the fighting was spiraling out of control, and he testily told an aide, "I am not prepared to bring on a general engagement today."

When he saw Hancock's troops were on the brink of being swept off the hill, however, he quickly changed his mind. One more push and Lee's army would control all of the high ground around Gettysburg. He sent an urgent message to Ewell, telling him, "It is only necessary to press those people in order to secure possession of the heights." Ewell, however, made no move, and the Union forces were able to strengthen their defensive positions.

General Robert E. Lee, 1807-1870

★ ★ ★ ★ ★

The Civil War produced many great figures, but none emerged as heroic as Robert E. Lee. Tall, handsome, and dignified—with a perfect military bearing—he was a brilliant field commander who was courteous in both victory and defeat.

Lee graduated from West Point in 1829, and later served as superintendent of the academy for a few years. He was decorated for bravery in the War with Mexico (1846-1848).

When the Civil War began in April 1861, Lee was offered command of the U.S. Army. He turned down the offer, saying he could not fight his own state (Virginia). Instead, he became a general in the Confederate army.

Lee named his force the Army of Northern Virginia, and over the next year, led it to several victories. By the Battle of Gettysburg, Southern troops—and Lee himself—had come to feel they couldn't be beaten. The costly defeat at Gettysburg destroyed that belief.

For the next twenty-one months, Lee could only postpone the inevitable, fighting defensive battles before finally surrendering to General Ulysses S. Grant in April of 1865. After the war, he encouraged his fellow Southerners to accept the defeat and work to restore unity. He became the president of Washington College, which was renamed "Washington and Lee" after his death. Lee suffered from heart disease for several years and died in 1870, only five years after the war.

By nightfall, the men on both sides were exhausted. The Union troops controlled Culp's Hill, Cemetery Hill, and Cemetery Ridge. The Confederates had established positions on Seminary Ridge. There was now a valley between the two armies less than a mile wide.

The losses on both sides had been staggering. The North's Iron Brigade, for example, had started the day with 1,829 men; 1,153 were casualties or prisoners by the end of the day. On the Confederate side, one regiment lost nearly 600 out of 800 men—killed, wounded, or missing.

General Winfield Scott Hancock helped the Union army establish defensive lines on the first day.

Gettysburg: Day 2

As the early morning mists slowly lifted on July 2, General Lee rode his famous horse, Traveller, along Seminary Ridge, studying the battle-field. He didn't like what he saw. Instead of Hancock's Union soldiers barely hanging on to Cemetery Ridge, Lee could now see the morning sun glistening off the barrels of Union cannons and rifles. The main part of the Army of the Potomac had arrived during the night, and General Meade had now established Union troops in a solid defensive arc, stretching from Culp's Hill and Cemetery Hill in the north to Little Round Top in the south, a distance of more than three miles.

"The enemy have the advantage of us in a shorter line," Lee said when General Longstreet joined him, "and we are too far extended."

The South's line, centered on Missionary Ridge, was two miles longer than the Union line. This meant that the Confederates were spread out much more thinly. It also meant that Meade could move men or artillery to trouble spots far more easily than Lee could.

Despite the difficulties, Lee was determined to attack. Longstreet, who had not arrived in time for the first day's fighting, argued vigorously against attacking. Instead, he urged Lee to move the Rebels around Meade's flank and establish a position between the Union army and Washington. Longstreet felt that this would make Meade fight on Lee's terms.

"The enemy have the advantage ... we are too far extended."

—*Confederate General Lee on the morning of July 2*

17

Confederate troops attacked from the base of Culp's Hill late on the second day.

Lee would not consider a change of plans. The morale of his men was high, and he felt that the move Longstreet suggested would seem like a retreat. The Rebels knew, probably better than Longstreet, how close they had come to smashing the Union army the day before. They would have agreed with Lee's blunt statement, "The enemy is there, and I am going to attack him there." Lee's battle plan called for Longstreet's divisions to attack the Union's that were positioned to the left on Cemetery Ridge, and for Ewell's men to attack their right. He expected Longstreet to begin the attack by noon, but it was after 4 P.M. before he had his men in position.

The delay irritated Lee, and his frustration grew when Jeb Stuart arrived. Stuart's cavalry was still miles away, so they would not be of much use. The best Lee could do was to order Stuart to go back to his men and try to attack Meade's supply lines the next day. The two men who Lee relied on most—Longstreet and Stuart—did not give him the support he needed in the most important battle of his career—perhaps the most decisive battle of the war.

During the long lull in the fighting, Union General Dan Sickles decided he did not like the position his division had been assigned

General George Meade, 1815-1872

★ ★ ★ ★ ★

George Meade succeeded by doing what was needed in a steady, colorless way. After graduating from West Point in 1835, he was out of the military for a few years, working as a surveyor and engineer. He returned to the army in 1842 and was decorated for bravery during the Mexican War (1846–1848). When the Civil War began, he was assigned to the Army of the Potomac and became corps commander late in 1862.

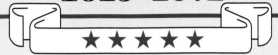

When President Lincoln chose him to command the Army of the Potomac in June 1863, Meade was reluctant to accept the promotion, but did so out of loyalty. With no time to develop a better strategy, he and his army performed brilliantly throughout the Battle of Gettysburg with defensive moves that blunted Rebel attacks. Although often criticized for not following through, Meade gave the North a decisive victory.

Meade commanded the Army of the Potomac until the end of the war. In 1864, General Ulysses S. Grant was named commander-in-chief of all Union armies, and established his headquarters with the Army of the Potomac. Another general might have disliked having the commander peering over his shoulder, but Meade displayed loyalty to Grant and to the Union. Meade remained with the army until shortly before his death in 1872 of an illness aggravated by a war wound.

on a low section of Cemetery Ridge. Without consulting Meade, he moved his men forward a half mile to higher ground. Without realizing it, Sickles had created a "salient," or bulge, in the Union line that almost cut off his division from the others.

Longstreet's Confederate division commanders quickly saw the mistake and unleashed an artillery barrage on Sickles' exposed position. The Rebels then rushed in to attack. One division veered into an area called the "Devil's Den"—a strange, haunting gully strewn with huge, jagged boulders. Union troops, well protected behind the boulders, cut down scores of the attackers. The Rebels kept coming, however, and the two sides clashed in vicious hand-to-hand fighting.

An Alabama brigade, led by Colonel William Oates, swept around the Devil's Den and started up Big Round Top. Oates immediately saw that nearby Little Round Top seemed to be deserted and ordered his 500 men to head for it. He felt that Little Round Top might hold the key position to the entire battlefield. If Confederate artillery could be moved onto that hill, they could fire on the entire Union line all the way to Culp's Hill.

General Robert E. Lee on his beloved horse, Traveller.

As Oates' men headed up the steep hillside, one of Meade's staff officers saw that the hill was undefended. He quickly found two brigades to rush to Little Round Top, including the 20th Maine, commanded by Colonel Joshua Chamberlain. The resulting clash became one of the most famous small-scale encounters of the war.

As the troops of the 15th Alabama reached the crest of Little Round Top, they were shocked to see Chamberlain's men already there. One of the Maine soldiers later wrote that the fighting became ". . . a terrible medley of cries, shouts, cheers, groans, prayers, curses, bursting shells, whizzing rifle bullets, and clanging steel . . . . The lines were so near each other that the hostile gun barrels almost touched."

On the Confederate side, Oates said, "My line wavered like a man trying to walk against a strong wind." Chamberlain, the Union commander, who a few months earlier had been a college professor, described how he came to make a bold decision to counter-attack: "They were close to us," Chamberlain recalled, "advancing rapidly, and firing as they came. We expended our last cartridge. I saw that there was no other way to save [the hill] or even ourselves, but to charge with the bayonet."

His Federals quickly attached bayonets to their empty rifles. When he gave the order, they rushed down the hill, yelling wildly, and charging into the startled Alabamans. The Rebels stumbled backward, turned, and ran or surrendered. Little Round Top remained in Union hands.

Farther north, as the fighting in the Devil's Den died down, another Rebel regiment charged into Sickles' troops in two areas that became known as the "Wheatfield" and the "Peach Orchard." With a terrifying "Rebel yell," more than 1,600 Confederates rushed the Union line.

The Rebels overtook the Peach Orchard, pausing only long enough to take 1,000 prisoners, then continued up Cemetery Ridge. Just as the courageous charge reached the top, three fresh Union divisions arrived and stopped the attack with artillery blasts at short range.

Bloody hand-to-hand fighting killed thousands on Little Round Top.

"...a terrible medley of cries, shouts, cheers, groans, prayers, curses, bursting shells, whizzing rifle bullets, and clanging steel.... The lines were so near each other that the hostile gun barrels almost touched."

A Maine soldier writing about the fighting

General James Longstreet was one of Lee's closest advisors.

The fighting raged back and forth for the rest of the day. One Confederate charge after another came close to breaking the Union lines, only to be stopped by the arrival of Union reinforcements. When the last Rebel tide receded, Longstreet said, "I do not hesitate to pronounce this the best three hours' fighting ever done by any troops on any battlefield." Longstreet had to admit, however, that the South had gained nothing, and his corps had suffered roughly 7,000 casualties out of the 22,000 men involved—nearly one-third of his force was killed, wounded, or missing.

As darkness fell, the men in Ewell's corps tried to take the Union positions on Culp's Hill and Cemetery Hill. Here, too, the Rebels were on the verge of a breakthrough but were stopped by the arrival of fresh Union troops. Around midnight, the Southerners had only a foothold on Culp's Hill and could not move forward or back.

That night, General Meade called his twelve generals together for advice on what to do. He had now been in command of Union forces for less than a week. He had had little time to sleep. And his army had already suffered some 15,000 casualties. So he was pleased when all twelve men agreed with his plan to stay in position and finish the fight the next day.

In the Confederate camp, Lee had also made up his mind. Once again, he was struck by how close his men had come to crushing the Army of the Potomac. Surely, Lee thought, with better timing and the effective use of artillery, his troops would win the battle.

★

Fighting lasted until midnight on July 2, with the Rebels failing to force the Union forces out of their strong defensive positions.

★

Gettysburg: Day 3

On July 3, the crash of Union artillery fire began soon after dawn as Meade's troops renewed the fighting on Culp's Hill and Cemetery Hill. When Lee heard the cannons, he knew his hope of attacking the Army of the Potomac on two fronts at once was ruined.

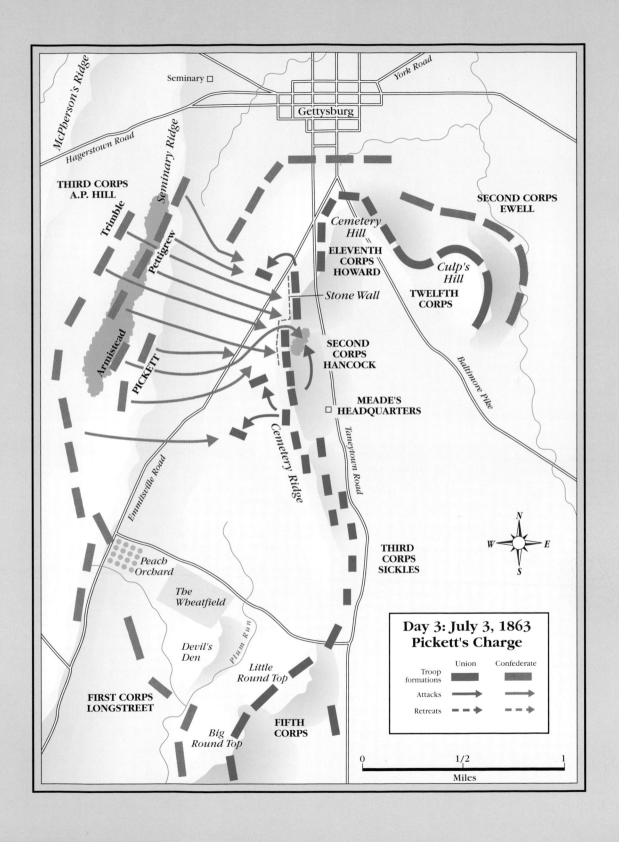

Seminary □

York Road

Gettysburg

McPherson's Ridge

Hagerstown Road

**THIRD CORPS
A.P. HILL**

Seminary Ridge

Trimble

Pettigrew

Armistead

PICKETT

*Cemetery
Hill*

**ELEVENTH
CORPS
HOWARD**

Stone Wall

**SECOND CORPS
EWELL**

*Culp's
Hill*

**TWELFTH
CORPS**

**SECOND
CORPS
HANCOCK**

Baltimore Pike

□ **MEADE'S
HEADQUARTERS**

Cemetery Ridge

Taneytown Road

Emmitsville Road

**THIRD
CORPS
SICKLES**

N
W · E
S

Peach
Orchard

*The
Wheatfield*

Plum Run

*Devil's
Den*

*Little
Round Top*

**FIRST CORPS
LONGSTREET**

*Big
Round Top*

**FIFTH
CORPS**

Day 3: July 3, 1863
Pickett's Charge

	Union	Confederate
Troop formations		
Attacks		
Retreats		

0   1/2   1

Miles

Confederates waited for the artillery duel to end before charging on day 3.

By mid-morning, Ewell's Rebels gave up trying to take either hill, and the entire battlefield fell silent.

The Southerners' hopes now depended on Longstreet's I Corps, even though two of his divisions had been battered the day before. When Lee showed Longstreet where he was to attack with 15,000 men—across the valley to the center of the Union line on Cemetery Ridge—Longstreet was horrified. "General, I have been a soldier all my life," Longstreet said. "It is my opinion that no 15,000 men . . . can take that position." Lee would not budge, although he agreed to remove some of Longstreet's men who were in no condition to fight. There would be 12,000 Confederates instead of 15,000. Half that number was a new division commanded by General George E. Pickett, which had not yet seen action at Gettysburg. Pickett was probably best known for his long, curled beard, and hair that fell to his shoulders in perfumed ringlets. But he was also known as a brave soldier who had the unquestioned loyalty of his men.

Longstreet's divisions began organizing in thick woods near the Peach Orchard. For more than two hours, soldiers on both sides suffered in the stifling heat, waiting for the eerie silence to end. At 1 P.M., the Confederate artillery opened fire on Cemetery Ridge—140 cannons from all three divisions, each gun with more than 130 rounds of ammunition. As dense smoke settled over the ridge and the valley, the Union's cannons responded. The artillery duel, the largest in the nation's history, continued steadily for more than two hours.

Longstreet hoped that the artillery would blast huge gaps in the Union lines to give his infantry a chance. But the bombardment didn't create nearly as much damage as he'd expected, partly because the ridge became hidden by cannon smoke and many Rebel shells sailed over the Union crest where they inflicted only minor damage.

At about 3 P.M., the Union artillery gradually subsided. Union officers hoped this would convince the Confederates that the cannons were being knocked out by Longstreet's bombardment. The trick worked. A Rebel artillery commander sent an urgent note to Pickett, telling him to start his attack while there was still some ammunition left.

Pickett rode over to Longstreet, repeated the message, and asked, "General, shall I advance?"

★

Confederate artillery began firing at Union lines in early afternoon, July 3.

★

A dead Confederate soldier lies among the rocks at Devil's Den.

General Meade met with officers under his command to plan day 3 of the battle.

Longstreet could not bring himself to give the order. He shifted in his saddle and looked away. Pickett understood. "I am going to move forward, sir," he said. Pickett rode back to his men and gave the order. All three Confederate divisions moved out of the woods into the searing heat. The commanders passed the word for the men not to shoot or to use their Rebel yell until ordered.

As Pickett's gray-clad Rebel troops crossed the valley—walking at a fast pace that was nearly a jog—they ran into deadly flanking fire from artillery on the Round Tops. The shells tore into the Confederate ranks "with fearful effect," a Union officer recalled, "sometimes as many as ten men being killed or wounded by the bursting of a single shell."

As men fell, the Rebels closed ranks and kept moving forward. Many followed General Lewis Armistead who advanced on foot, holding his sword aloft with his black hat perched on top of it.

Then the mass of men in gray approached a low stone wall, not seeing the Union defenders crouched behind it. When the Confederates were less than 200 yards away, the Union commander shouted, "Fire!" Instantly, 11 cannons and 1,700 rifles opened fire on the Confederate attackers. The Rebel lines were staggered, but the survivors kept advancing. With 100 yards to go, the Confederates heard the order to

"Come on, boys! Give them cold steel! Who will follow me?"

General Lewis Armistead

26

stop and fire, unleashing a volley that shattered part of the Union line. One artillery battery was knocked out and hundreds of Union soldiers in one division broke and fled.

Several hundred Confederates managed to reach the stone wall and swarmed over it. The only leader to make it that far was Armistead. Still holding up his sword and hat, he shouted, "Come on, boys! Give them cold steel! Who will follow me?"

The men behind him responded with the spine-tingling Rebel yell.

The Union troops were close to breaking. At this instant, the Confederacy reached its "high water mark"—like the crest of a wave. Never again would the South come so close to winning the battle, the war, or the independence of the Confederate States of America.

General George Pickett ordered the most famous charge of the Civil War.

That crest lasted only seconds. In the next instant, Armistead fell with a fatal gunshot wound and Northern reinforcements crashed into the Rebels. The two disorganized masses stood toe-to-toe— shooting, bayoneting, and clubbing. Without a leader to rally them, every Rebel who reached the top was killed, wounded, or captured within minutes. The men behind began backing down the slope. Some Union officers tried to launch a counter-attack, but the troops refused to move. They could fight no more that day.

As the defeated Confederates staggered back to their lines, a shattered General Lee rode among them on Traveller, trying to offer encouragement. As Pickett rode up, badly shaken, Lee urged him to organize his men. With tears streaming down his face, Pickett replied, "General Lee, I have no division now."

"Come, General Pickett," Lee said softly. "Your men have done all that men can do. The fault is entirely my own."

On July 3, Confederates reached the top of Cemetery Ridge in late afternoon and were immediately driven back, ending the battle.

The Aftermath

The next day, July 4, the skies opened in a great deluge, as if the rains wanted to wash away all the blood spilled in the grim three days before. Lee began organizing his battered army for the long march back

27

The Soldiers of 1863

A Union private wrote that a soldier's daily life was "99 percent boredom and one percent sheer terror." Whether a soldier wore a Union or Confederate uniform, those words were true. Here is a look at the foot soldiers who fought the Civil War.

Confederates wore short-waist jackets and pants made of heavy "jean" type material. Because the uniforms were dyed by several different methods, the colors were a mix of grays and browns. Federals called Confederates "butternuts" because of

Union soldier

the color of the uniforms. Shirts and undergarments were made of cotton and were usually sent from home. Southern-made shoes wore out quickly and were difficult to replace.

Northern uniforms were high-quality wool—warm in the winter, but itchy and uncomfortable in Southern heat. They were dyed dark blue until 1862 when the pants were dyed a lighter shade of blue. The well-known cap, made of stiff wool with a leather visor, was worn by most soldiers. Like the Confederate troops, most Union soldiers hated the itchy wool army shirt and wore cotton shirts and underwear from home.

Every Union soldier carried between 30 and 40 pounds of gear. Besides his rifle, this gear was made up of a belt that held a cartridge box, bayonet, and scabbard. The soldier also carried a haversack for rations, a canteen, and a pack that held a wool blanket, a shelter half, and perhaps a rubber jacket. Inside his pack, a soldier carried a change of socks, writing paper, envelopes, ink and pen, and other personal items.

Confederate soldiers traveled light because they did not have the extras that Union soldiers carried. As the war dragged on, supplies grew scarcer. Equipment was difficult to replace and new clothing was rare for the enlisted man. In some battles, Confederates removed the shoes from the bodies of dead Federals to replace their worn out shoes.

With food, it was much the same. A Union food ration was meant to last three days and was basically salted pork and hard flour biscuits called hardtack. Hardtack, also called "worm castles" and "iron crackers" by the soldiers, could be eaten straight, though most men preferred to crumble them into soups or fry them with their pork and bacon fat. Rice, peas, beans, dried fruit, potatoes, molasses, and salt were other foods carried by troops. Of all the rations Union troops carried, however, coffee was the most popular. Soldiers even carried small coffee bean grinders.

Confederate soldier

Confederate soldiers lived on less rations than Union troops. Their diet consisted of bacon, cornmeal, molasses, peas, rice, and tobacco. Confederates also received a coffee substitute that was not as tasty as the real coffee of the Northerners. Between battles, when opposing sides were camped near each other, trades of tobacco for coffee were quite common between Federals and Rebels. Other items traded included newspapers, sewing needles, and buttons.

to Virginia. On the same day, at Vicksburg, Mississippi, Confederate General John C. Pemberton surrendered the city to Union General Grant, along with his entire Rebel army of 30,000 men.

To these 30,000 troops, the Confederacy had to add the men lost at Gettysburg. During the three days, the Army of Northern Virginia had suffered about 28,000 casualties—more than one-third of the force that had left Fredericksburg. More than half the Gettysburg casualties had been veterans—men who had been with Lee from the beginning. The loss of almost 60,000 men in the two battles was more than the South could bear; there was simply no way to replace them. The North's losses at Gettysburg had also been high—roughly 23,000 casualties—but the Union, with its much greater population, could replace that number.

Over the next two weeks, Lee led his men back toward Virginia. General Meade, with constant prodding from Washington, tried to organize his battle-weary Union troops to attack, but his men responded reluctantly. They finally caught up with the Army of Northern Virginia at the Potomac crossing, where rains had flooded the river and made it too difficult to cross.

On the morning of July 14, the Union troops were ready to attack, but they found only empty trenches. During the night, the river level had fallen enough for Lee's men to cross on a makeshift pontoon bridge which they destroyed behind them. Lee and his army had escaped to fight again. President Lincoln was distraught when he heard this. "We had them within our grasp," Lincoln said. "We had only to stretch forth our hands and they were ours. And nothing I could say or do could make the army move." Lincoln could not yet see how severely the Confederacy had been weakened by the combination of Gettysburg and Vicksburg. Never again would a Rebel army invade the North or even launch an offensive campaign. Although Lee's army remained intact, he could do little more than delay the inevitable by fighting and retreating until there was no more room to retreat. The end came at Appomatox Court House in April 1865, when Lee surrendered the remnants of his once invincible army to General Grant.

Glossary

artillery large weapons used by fighting forces that fall into three categories—guns or cannons, howitzers, and mortars

brigade a military unit smaller that a division, usually consisting of three to five regiments of 500 to 1,000 soldiers

cavalry combat troops on horses

commander a military leader, usually holding the rank of general

corps a military grouping of between 10,000 and 20,000 soldiers

division a military grouping of between 6,000 and 8,000 soldiers or two to three brigades

pontoon a float used in building a temporary bridge

quartermaster officer in charge of providing food, clothing, shelter, and other basic supplies

regiment a military unit smaller than brigade and a division. In the Civil War soldiers fought in the same regiment throughout the war with fellow soldiers from the same state, city, or town

reinforce in military terms, to strengthen a military unit by sending in fresh troops

For More Information

Books

Burgan, Michael. *The Battle of Gettysburg* (We the People). Glen Ridge, NJ: Compass Point, 2001.

Hughes, Christopher. *Gettysburg* (Battlefields Across America). Brookfield, CT: Twenty-First Century Book, 1998.

Murphy, Jim. *The Long Road to Gettysburg*. NY: Clarion Books, 2000.

Willis, Gary (editor). *The Gettysburg Address*. Boston, MA: Houghton Mifflin, Company, 1998.

Web Sites

Battle of Gettysburg
Learn more about the battle of Gettysburg and its aftermath—
www.militaryhistoryonline.com/gettysburg/default.htm

Gettysburg National Military Park
Visit and see pictures of the battlefield at Gettysburg, Pennsylvania—
www.nps.gov/gett

Index